DEALING

WITH

STUBBORN

DEBTORS

TELLA OLAYERI

08023583168

Published By:

GOD'S LINK VENTURES

Email tellaolayeri@gmail.com

Website www.tellaolayeri.com

US Contact
Ruth Jack
14 Milewood Road
Verbank
N.Y.12585
U.S.A. +19176428989

DEDICATION

This book is dedicated to the **HOLY GHOST** for inspiring me to write this eye opener book.

APPRECIATION

My appreciation goes to my dedicated wife, **MRS NGOZI OLAYERI,** who typed the manuscript of this book and design the cover page.

My darling wife I say thank you. My appreciation equally goes to my lovely children, **MISS IBUKUN, DAVID, MICHAEL, COMFORT and MERCY.** They encouraged me day and night as I write this book. Hurray, after seven years of research, reading, listening to counsels and support of the Holy Spirit etc. the long awaited book, bad dream enemies use to rob blessing and the way out is out!

Respect and honor should be given to who is due. Favor comes from God and men as well. My calling (writing evangelism) met the timely support of a particular man of God, preacher, teacher, prophet and General Overseer. He awakes my inner man, gave me sound spiritual support and stood by me in fulfillment of my calling.

This book you are holding is a testimony of my claim. This book wouldn't have seen the light of the day, if not for the spiritual encouragement I gathered from my father in the Lord who served as spiritual mirror that brightens my hope to explore my calling.

I am talking of no any other person than the **General Overseer of *MOUNTAIN OF FIRE AND MIRACLES MINISTRIES WORLD WIDE*, DR. D. K. OLUKOYA.**

Once again, I say thank you sir. Your support has yielded yet another earth shaking book.

THANKS

Evangelist Tella Olayeri.

PREFACE

This book teaches one how to live victoriously every day and not live a defeated life. You are here on earth for a specific assignment. Enemies will bring problems, evil agenda etc. to threaten your existence. We are confronted with different degrees of debtors, while some are co-operatives; some are stubborn and not willing to pay. Until you overcome situations that compound your finances or business, you may not break even.

This book stands out among books to address issues of debtors and creditors. It reveals new dimensions to recover money from unwilling debtors. There are keys to apply if you want your money paid time and in good faith. As good as it becomes visible that debtors are unwilling to pay.

This book is in-depth to address the issue. It focuses on both practical ways to collect your money and spiritual steps to take. This book is written to bring hope to thousands humiliated by debtors. There are cases of debtors who attack their creditors both in the spirit and in physical. Some want their debtors dead, bankrupt or financially crippled to avoid payment.

But there is hope in the horizon.

What makes this book unique is that a chapter is specifically written on how you will pray for your debtors to improve in their endeavour and pay. Debtors are not enemy but associate in business. Hence debtors pay, creditors feel happy and think ahead, and when they don't creditors finds it difficult to have favourable balance sheet. In order to avoid this, it is good you pray for them to have robust economy, and God to touch their heart to pay what they owe.

This book gives you opportunity to involve God in that you do. Debt payment is not easy mostly when it involves stubborn debtors. Here, this book gives a thorough blend on how to call on God through prayers. Prayer is a powerful tool in detecting the secrets to the issues of life. Prayer in this book shall take you to the supernatural realm where revelations are unfolded. The source of your problem and how to go about it will be exposed as you war in prayer.

The fact is this book is loaded with prayers that will turn your life around in the midst of financial conflict. It is good to have sound management style, so it is, to support it with prayer. As you know, prayer answers all things.

Brethren, I advise you to build hope and expect favourable turnaround in business and in career.

God shall see you through. Amen.

GOOD NEWS!!!

My audiobook is now available, to get one visit acx.com and search **"Tella Olayeri."**

Brethren, to be loaded and reloaded visit: *amazon.com/author/tellaolayeri* for a full spiritual sojourn for my books.

Thanks.

PREVIOUS PUBLICATIONS OF THE AUTHOR

1. 100% CONFESSIONS and PROPHECIES to Locate Helpers and helpers to locate you
2. 1000 Prayer Points for Children Breakthrough
3. 1010 (One Thousand and Ten) DREAMS and Interpretations
4. 2000 Dangerous Prayer for First Born
5. 365 DREAMS and INTERPRETATIONS
6. 430 Prayers to Cancel Bad Dreams and Overcome Witchcraft Powers part one (DREAMS AND YOU Book 1)
7. 430 Prayers to Claim Good Dreams and Overcome Witchcraft Powers part two (DREAMS AND YOU Book 2)
8. 630 Acidic Prayers: With Missile Prayer for Speedy Breakthrough, Healing and Deliverance
9. 650 DREAMS AND INTERPRETATIONS
10. 700 Prayers to Clear Unemployment Out of Your Way
11. 720 Missile Prayers that Silence Enemies: Prayers that Bring Peace and Rest
12. 740 Rocket Prayers that Break Satanic Embargo
13. 777 Deliverance Prayers for Healing and Breakthrough
14. 800 Deliverance Prayer for Middle Born: Daily Devotional for Teen and Adult

See all at: amazon.com/author/tellaolayeri

Table of Contents

CHAPTER ONE

WHY DEBTORS OWE

Debtors are people that buy goods from producers, middle men or people with intention to pay in the nearest future day, month, or year as the case may be. To sell on credit is one major way to business robust. As good as it is, most people or corporate body that buy on credit are unwilling to pay. Once the product or service is delivered on credit, most receivers don't like to pay, while some drag legs, others don't like to pay at all, until hell is let loose.

Debtors are categorised into eight folds as follows:

1. A debtor can be a company.
2. A debtor can be a friend.
3. A debtor can be a family member.
4. A debtor can be a stranger.
5. A debtor can be a business associate.
6. A debtor can be a neighbour you know.
7. A debtor can be a nation
8. A debtor can be a spirit.

The last category is not common but it exists. This is a situation when one works in the spirit or in a dream but is denied payment. Such person serves a spirit slave master. He uses the souls of people to expand his wealth in the spirit.

Also, there are different categories of debtors. These are debtors that form strange habit after they bought good or receive service but refuse to pay.

They can be grouped into the following:

1. Stubborn debtors.
    These are debtors that made up their minds not to pay what they owe. They buy on credit, but choose to be difficult once the goods or service are received.
2. Charmed debtors.
    These are debtors that are cursed. They are under spell. They find it difficult to account for money that comes their way. They spend all, no matter how large the money they receive.
3. Confused debtors.
    These are debtors willing to pay, but ill advised by friends or people not to pay their bills.
4. Situational debtors.
    These are debtors who don't like to owe but for reasons they become debtors. They owe either because they are sacked in office, their

source of livelihood stopped, as their shops either burned, demolished or their goods seized or stolen.

5. Inheritance debtors.

These are debtors that are not the original debtor. They inherited the debt either from spouse, children, parents, or friends they stood in gap for. An example in the bible is the widow of Shunammite whose late husband's creditor was about to take her two sons as slaves because her late husband couldn't pay before he died. The woman was poor and couldn't pay. It was in this condition prophet Elisha appeared in her life. 2Kings 4: 1-7.

6. Sick debtors.

These are debtors who wish to pay their debt, but due to ill-health, they are on sick bed or incapacitated to function and unable to raise money to feed or pay what they owe. Some debtors' condition is so critical that when creditor goes after them, he will pity the debtor and support him with aide in food or money to feed or take care of himself!

7. Dead debtors.

These are debtors that die and couldn't be reached for payment before they die. In such situation, he has no guarantor or someone that can be approached for payment.

8. Stubborn debtors.

These are debtors that refuse to pay even they have money to do the needful. They prefer to dodge their creditors anytime he calls, or go after the life of the creditor by sending assassin to him, visit witch doctors to harm the creditor or find foul means to attack the creditor.

These last categories of debtor are wicked and are common in the society today. They boast at the creditor, that they won't pay. They at times threaten their creditors to his face. They become rascals after they received the goods or services. Their mission is not to pay what they owe.

Really, some debts are not ordinary. Debt comes in several ways. There are people who never dreamt to be a debtor but for reasons far beyond them. Such people find it difficult to explain what happen before situation change for worse. Such people may suffer any of the followings:-

1. **When a person packed to a newly rented house that is evil**. There are houses that can best be described as evil or satanic house. The

day you move into such house, announced your day of doom. Things will start to change in the negative, before you know it, it is either you or your children fall sick thereby drain your pocket. At times, many sold their properties and leave!

2. **Another reason is when you are fired arrow of failure or sickness**. Such arrow paralyses finance. Any form of evil against such person drains the pocket and eventually leads to bankruptcy and turn victim to debtor.

3. **When you leave good office for demonic or less attractive job** felt was good enough to promote your finance. After you leave your previous job, then you realise your mistake. Remember not all that glitter is gold.

4. Another way many go bankrupt or indebted is **when they reveal their business secret to wrong hands.** Once the secret is known, it will be used against them. This will affect his source of wealth and eventually erode his finance. If care is not taken, he may go bankrupt and find it difficult to meet formal obligations. Since his source of income is under threat, he becomes a debtor.

5. Another way is **when you buy what you don't really need**. There are people who go for

ostentatious goods they don't need. They buy it to show off in the society, such goods drain their pocket and put them in debt.

6. **If you offend God**. Sin is abomination before God. It is a disaster to turn your back at God because of what the world had to offer you. What is that thing in your life that is restricting you from following Christ? Don't do things contrary to God's rule or demand. If you do, Satan will unseat you and scatter your source of income. Your money in the hands of debtor becomes prime point of attack. If debtors fail to pay, you are confused because you won't know the next step to take.

7. **If you fail to maintain good financial record with debtors**. Financial records in terms of invoices issued, ledger kept, profit and loss records and other book of entries are important. If either side, mostly creditors fail to keep good record, debtors may find it easy to evade payment. Therefore, keep good financial record, and keep your debtor in touch.

8. **If you join cult, and or, wants to withdraw**. Cult is a witchcraft association. They don't take Jesus as their personal Lord and saviour. When a debtor or creditor is a member, and withdraw membership, his finance, business or career

may be attacked. Once this is done, unexplainable losses, attacks and evil may prevail in his life. The effect is blockage and failure in business and career. Thus, to meet up bills become a problem.

9. **If you operate a bewitched account.** Account can be bewitched by workers, children, friends, debtors etc. Once an account is bewitched errors will multiply, while at times, document may miss. If any of these happen, it may lead to irreconcilable account, thereby breed mistrust, anger, quarrel and eventual non-payment of money owed.

10. **Attack of the idol of your father's house**. Every idol of your father's house has agenda. There are agenda not to succeed, agenda of failure at the edge of breakthrough etc. Many die young as a result of the power of their father's house, some lose out rightly when the horizon is clear for them to progress. Some are pulled down when they are about to grow financially. All this boiled down to non-payment of debt by debtors because of unseen hands playing witchcraft roles in the system.

11. **Stubbornness and pride of debtors.** If a debtor is proud and un-co-operative, it may be difficult to pay what he owe. If the creditor is

proud and can't go after debtors, he will be owed. Pride can therefore swell up debt.

12. **If evil arrow is fired against a good**. When a good is fired arrow, it becomes unattractive for sale. When money doesn't come in, losses are recorded, thereby makes it impossible to pay what is owed.

13. **Act of God**. Act of God is unquestionable. It happens without human contribution to it.

    Most debtors are happy when their creditors die. Some lie and never pay what they owe. It is called Act of God. Examples are fire outbreak, flood, lightening etc. When such happens, goods may be lost and thereby leads to non-payment of money owed.

14. **Unnecessary business intimacy.** When you allow family and friends overcrowd or take over your business, they hardly pay when they buy. They ruin business and look elsewhere when you go bankrupt. To avoid this, ensure you do business as usual in business manner with both friends and relatives. The simple rule should be, "buy and pay". Treat them the way you will treat normal business associates.

15. **Untimely death of either party.** If either party dies, it is always difficult for other party to pay,

mostly when the business is not a going concern.

16. **Inability to interpret dreams**. Your dream has meaning, don't look down on it. Dream may tell you what is about to happen, what happened in the past or what may happen in future. If you decode your dream and interpret it well, you may have warning dream that tells you to curtail the way you do business with people. This may save you from incurring loss as a result non-payment of money owed.

17. **Prayerlessness.** This is the area most creditors fail to address. Put God first in what you do. If God is on your side, problems and financial catastrophe will be far from you.

    With prayer, debtor's hearts are arrested to pay up their debts and co-operative with creditors. On the other hand, if you don't pray, there may be crack in the wall, that may allow Satan dominate your business. Once this is allowed, debtors will have free hand to operate and scatter your business.

CHAPTER TWO

TWENTY EFFECTIVE WAYS TO PERSUADE DEBTORS TO PAY

In business, it is allowed to sell goods on credit, but it shouldn't be a condition. Let it be last resort after much persuasion from would-be-debtor. The beginning is always simple and friendly, but often goes sour when debtors find it difficult to pay or refuse to pay.

It may be easy in a well-structured society, but difficult in developing countries where voodoo and juju, are used against creditors, and or, assassins sent after creditors. These uncivil acts have sent many to untimely grave. For this reason, we shall approach this subject in a broad way. Approaches to it are many, but we shall treat them step by step as follows:

1. **Apply effective Credit Control method.**
   This is the first bridge to build and cross in debtors control system. Build effective credit control and query management to enable your business; improve in cash flow, reduce debtor days, increase customer service, cut the cost of cash collection,

eliminate manual process, and speed up the query resolution process.

For timely collection, a system is designed called ***early warning system***. It is a computer based auto-system. It will show on daily basis the debts which has become due but not received. On the basis of this report, you will contact debtors immediately through phone or letter to pay.

Warning! Pursue debtors timely. The older a debt becomes the less collective it will be.

2. **Charge interests on late payment.**

   Whenever creditor-debtor relationship is established, ensure you charge interest to discourage debtor to stay back payment. Debtors will be discouraged to owe or accumulate more debt if he knows interest will be charged on unpaid transactions. You can encourage your customers to pay their debts early enough, if you apply the rule, "pay quick and on due date if you don't want to add interest to your bill". Once you agree on this, every debtor will like to pay their bills quickly to avoid added cost.

3. **Call for a guarantor.**

   A guarantor in the face of transaction makes business flow unhindered. A guarantor stays in gap if the debtor fails to pay what owed. For this reason, before you offer anyone loan or credit, you must ensure they have a third party who would guarantee the debt and offer to pay when the debtor can't. This is helpful to ensure your funds are safe as the guarantor will pay if the debtor fails. Your business and finance is laminated against bankruptcy, as in either way, someone will pay the bill or debt.

4. **Establish robust payment terms.**

   This is a very good step to take if creditors want debtors to pay on time. What you will do, is to draw suitable options of two or three for debtors to pick from. By this he will be bound with the option he picks. This shows there is understanding of interest between both parties. At this point, default may be dangerous as you allow him "shoot his legs" in the beginning.

5. **Understand law that guides debt collection**.

   There is no ignorance in law. To avoid being on the receiving side in case of court action, know the rules of the game. Make sure you know law that guide the type of business you operate. Find out what the law says about debt collection in your own country before you set out, so that you can avoid doing anything that would land you in trouble.

6. **Set a deadline.**

Determine when you will start to take action against the debtor. This depends on the value of the good or amount owed. You may have time limit for small value, and another for big value items. At times, specific time duration applies to all debtors.

Whichever is the time deadline, ensure you follow it to the letter. Above all, apply diplomacy when you go after your debtors to avoid sour relationship. The rule is, ensure you pursue your debtor for repayment after the time deadline lapses.

7. **Send reminders.**

Contact your debtors with a gentle reminder when the time deadline set lapses. Let your first contact with the debtor be in the form of a gentle reminder, either by a mail or on the phone. Such reminder makes him save face, as he may claim he "didn't know" or "forgot". At this stage, a certain percentage of debtors pay as soon as they know or are reminded. These are debtors with conscience.

There are some debtors who choose to ignore reminders. To this set of debtors, you may need to send several reminders that will touch their heart for payment; your language may be soft in the initial, but get stern but polite in subsequent reminders.

8. **Apply persuasion method**.

    It is not always easy to contact people about paying you money they owe, because they may resist or be violent; respond in anger or come with nasty argument. Above all, it is more pleasant to use the art of persuasion.

    When you approach a debtor, put in a friendly move. You can start this by, starting your conversation with debtor by asking why he hadn't pay. This method covers all strata of debtors from low income to high income earners.

    The reason may be much depending on the debtor in question. It spans from, job loss, car repairs, fighting illness that drains financial resources. To others, they don't know how to handle their money responsibly. You do this, to show you are concerned about them they are happy and their heart melt to pay.

9. **Call at the right time.**

One good method is to call your debtor at the right time he will pick call and answer you well. Avoid riot to call at odd time, like middle of the night, very early in the morning or where it will be difficult to pick calls. Also, you can also leave voice messages if you are finding it hard to reach a debtor on phone.

One good method is to call your debtor when in office. This method is good because he is most likely to tell someone that cares to listen that he is owes and looking for a way out. In such situation, help may come. But then, let the step you take be tactical, to avoid being liable for significant civil damages. Don't discuss his debt with anyone else or do anything that may jeopardise his job.

10. **Adopt prioritisation of payment**.

It is good to approach and convince your debtor if he refuses to pay. You can work hand in hand to put yours in his list of top priority. Hence, you constantly contact him by phone, by letters, through the e-mail, and may be by knocking on his door. Your persistence may pay off.

11. **Keep your attitude in check.**

Your attitude counts when it comes to debt collection. Debtors are not easy kernel to crack when debt collection is in question. You must not be rude or nasty to debtors when you approach them to pay debt. Don't take it personal but be diplomatic in your approach. Appeal to your debtor to pay, it is when all fail you can approach your lawyer.

12. **Apply carrot-stick method.**

In every step you take, make good relationship with your customer and employ good communication skill. The carrot-stick approach may include offering them deals that hasten payment. Such deals may include among others; a special discount may be offered to ease the debt collection or offer some kind of incentives which would encourage them to pay off debts.

13. **Accept instalmental payments.**

You must not be harsh on your customer when it is clear he is finding it difficult to pay. Though collection of debt method varies, you should give room for instalmental payment to ease payment. Your agreement and payment terms should be established around instalmental payments.

14. **Wear garment of patience.**

In every business deal that involves debtor-creditor relationship, patience is the mother of all business. You must be patient in how you handle matters with your debtors, but at the same time persistent about collecting your debt.

If this gentleman method fails, it is good you demand payment. Here you must be civil and not hostile to your debtor. What you will do is, make it clear to him you are rightly owed the money and you need payment, and or, tell exact time or day he will pay the money.

This is a crucial point in debt payment history. At this point, weigh the reasons for non-payment. If you observe the debtor can still be "pardoned" for a while, you can be patient. But if you are sure the debtor is a chronic and unrepentant one, it is better you become morally aggressive to collect your money. If this fails again, you may approach a lawyer.

15. **Hire a professional.**

You can approach a licensed and bonded collection agency whose service include consumer and commercial collections, judgement recovery, skip tracing services, and flat fees collections. They will be your eyes and ears in business. They make the process simple, let your account simple and user friendly, while your files are in safe hands so that you put your focus back on duties that will help you succeed.

Hiring a third party to conduct your claims lets the debtor know you are serious. But then, since they will charge some percentage of what you are paid, check it with if the partial payment is better than nothing.

16. **Threaten to inform credit bureaus.**

Everyone wants to have good credit rating to continue in business. Good credit rating stands as goodwill in case of reference. If you are noted as a chronic debtor, nobody will like to associate with you. To avoid this, most debtors won't like their name mired with negatives. So, if you threaten a debtor with credit bureau, he may have a change of mind to pay. You might start receiving payment, as if on a platter of gold!

17. **Accept assets in place of cash.**

Decide if you will accept alternative forms of payments. In a situation you know collecting money may be difficult, let the debtor provide something else in return. If providing a favour or service will do, accept it, but don't be too quick to bargain as he may take advantage and negotiate it down.

Here, you will put diplomatic pressure on your debtor to surrender their asset in lieu of cash payment. Really, most debtors wont readily agree, but with persuasion and built of trust, he may surrender it.

18. **File a law suit.**

You can employ the service of a law firm if you observe your debtor is unyielding to pay his debt. This is always a man to man, or a woman and corporate, last step to take when all efforts failed.

19. **Dream interpretation.**

Remember and know how to interpret your dreams. This may look awkward in real sense, but it matters. Your dream may reveal the character of your debtor at initial stage of business. It may be a warning dream that informs you not to sell further to a particular debtor any longer. Dreams can reveal, the debtor is seeking other means or gods to attack or eliminate you. Dream can tell you to stop business with a particular debtor or person, as danger is in the offing.

The following dreams signals danger either in finance or in the life of the dreamer. We shall mention just a few; but if you want to know more, buy my book titled DICTIONARY OF DREAMS. This book has over ten thousand dreams and interpretations. It will help you unravel issues that relate to life, business, career and daily activity.

i.   If you are pursued by masquerade in the dream, know that dark spiritual forces is after you not to reap what you sow.

ii. If you walk barefooted in the dream, it portends ill-luck, poverty and stagnancy. In such situation know the type of people you mix business with.

iii. If you find yourself in the forest, almost lost or unable to find your way out until you wake from sleep. This means there is agenda of darkness in your life. There may be confusion in what you lay hands on at this material time.

iv. If you are naked in the dream, it foretells arrow of wickedness is fired against you, or you lay hands on unprofitable ventures. Beware of friends you keep, and or, the business you do.

v.	If you experience drought in the dream, it foretells unexplained failure in business or career in the offing.

vi.	If your roof leaks in the dream, it foretells problems arising that may affect your purse and eventual loss in business.

vii.	If you are a slave in the dream, it portends, work without privilege, arrow of slavery, and poverty is fired against you. It suggests your business is under attack.

viii.	If you are in chain in the dream, it foretells arrow of stagnancy and failure at the end of the tunnel.

ix.	If your certificate is toured in the dream. It suggests sack in office, business failure and poverty in the offing.

x.	If you fall from great height in the dream; it suggests sudden failure in business after much effort is exerted. Also, shame, poverty and inability to collect what debtors owe are prevalent.

xi.	If you see sealed padlock in the dream; it suggest failure at the edge of breakthrough, destiny attack and arrow of stagnancy.

xii.	If your house, goods or business is razed down in the dream, it suggests prominent failure in business and trade. Arrow of poverty and stagnancy etc.

20. **Go on your kneels**

Prayer open doors you list expect. It can touch the heart of stubborn, wicked, arrogant and irreconcilable debtors. There stone hearts will melt before violent and acidic prayers. They will change their evil thought against creditor and pay. The magic behind it, is prayer.

When you pray, mountain melts, slippery way expires, gully roads are filled and levelled, dark clouds that causes financial epilepsy disappear, cry turn to joy, bankruptcy gives way to breakthrough, as debtors pay their bills. They settle their accounts with smiles.

The simple reason is, God arises in his throne, and turn impossibility to possibility. To achieve this, we shall go into prayer proper in the next chapter.

CHAPTER THREE

OH HEAVEN LISTEN TO MY PRAYER

Psalm 91:11. "For he will command his angels concerning you to guard you in all your ways; they will lift you up in their hands, so that you will not strike your foot against a stone."

Psalm 64:1-2. "Hear me, O God, as I voice my complaint; protect my life from the threat of the enemy, hide me from the conspiracy of the wicked, from that noisy crowd of evildoers."

1. Oh heaven open, listen to my prayer today and answer me in the name of Jesus

2. O Lord, forgive me the sins that will delay my prayer to ascend to the throne of God in the name of Jesus

3. O Lord, forgive me the sins that will not let me receive favour and mercy, from the throne of God in the name of Jesus

4. Blood of Jesus, clear every obstacle on my way in the name of Jesus.

5. Blood of Jesus, encircle me against attacks of darkness, in the name of Jesus.

6. I drink blood of Jesus, to enrich my health and purge me of impurity in my system, in the name of Jesus.

7. O Lord, give me spirit to do good, that will not be used to attack me, in the name of Jesus.

8. O Lord, let justice roll like a river against enemy of my breakthrough, in the name of Jesus.

9. O Lord, let my debtors see me as a helper, not as a fighter, so that their mind can be soft to pay me, in the name of Jesus.

10. Holy Ghost Power, revive my account and balance it in my favour, in the name of Jesus.

11. Angels of God, give every strongman in charge of my account dirty slap of confusion in the name of Jesus.

12. Every habitation of the wicked that is against my finance, catch fire and roast to ashes in the name of Jesus.

13. Lord Jesus, bless my vessel of breakthrough in the name of Jesus.

14. The ox knows his master, therefore my debtors remember me and pay me, in the name of Jesus

15. The donkey knows his owner's manger; therefore my debtors remember me and pay me, in the name of Jesus.

16. Any power that boast, I will not have peace, you are not my God, die in the name of Jesus.

17. O heaven, deliver me, untie rope of darkness in my hands, in the name of Jesus.

18.O heaven set me free from bondage of poverty in the name of Jesus.

19.O heaven, cause fear and panic in my debtors to pay me, in the name of Jesus.

20.My father and my God, silence evil accountants in charge of my account in the name of Jesus.

21.Spiritual powers delaying my prayer in the spirit die in the name of Jesus.

22.Every anti-testimony arrow fired against my prayer; backfire to the sender in the name of Jesus.

23.O Lord, roar like thunder and scatter the camp of my enemy in the name of Jesus.

24.Fire of deliverance go deep to my foundation and heal me, in the name of Jesus.

25.My home shall not be desolate in the name of Jesus.

26.My mouth shall be larger than my debtors in the name of Jesus.

27.Angels of heaven, fire back every arrow of demotion fired against me in the name of Jesus.

28.Angels of God, strike down desert spirit in charge of my affairs in the name of Jesus.

29.O Lord, settle every dispute between me and my debtors in the name of Jesus.

30.Holy Spirit, paralyse every hand debtors raise against me, in the name of Jesus.

31. O Lord, take away my disgrace in the name of Jesus.

32. O Lord, make my life beautiful and glorious in the name of Jesus.

33. O Lord, give me shelter and shade from the heat of the day, in the name of Jesus.

34. O Lord, give me protection from storm that naked destiny, in the name of Jesus.

35. Hands of God turn plants that yield bad fruits to plants of good fruits, in the name of Jesus.

36. O heaven, speak against every conspiracy against my finance, in the name of Jesus.

37. Anoint my head O Lord, and let my cup runneth over, in the name of Jesus.

38. O Lord, let heaven open and draw my debtors close to me, in the name of Jesus.

39. O Lord, expose and disgrace looters in the dark waiting to strike and scatter my finance in the name of Jesus.

40. O Lord, censor, stop and nullify activities of dark media sponsored against me in the name of Jesus.

41. O Lord, terminate groans in my life in the name of Jesus.

42. Oh heaven declare and support me; my enemies shall fall and rise no more, in the name of Jesus.

43. Oh heaven open, let me be a blessing to this world, in the name of Jesus.

44. O Lord, give me shelter from every storm against my destiny, in the name of Jesus.

45. Every destructive wind targeted against my career, scatter, in the name of Jesus.

46. Every flood downpour aimed at sinking my finance, oh heaven dry it up, in the name of Jesus.

47. O Lord, put your glorious crown upon me, in the name of Jesus.

48. Oh heaven, speak against every plot of the enemy to scatter my finance, in the name of Jesus.

49. I speak woe to those who visit witch doctor to harm me, in the name of Jesus.

50. Oh heaven, bless my barn of breakthrough in the name of Jesus.

51. Oh heaven, deliver my soul from spirit of Pharaoh, that use me as slave in the spirit, in the name of Jesus.

52. Hardship assign for me in the spirit, die in the name of Jesus.

53. Holy Spirit Divine, pour your spirit upon me in the name of Jesus.

54. Lord Jesus, turn my desert to fertile land in the name of Jesus.

55. I will live in peaceful and secured home in the name of Jesus.
56. My foundation, receive heavenly blessing in the name of Jesus.
57. O Lord arise, nullify every dark treaty signed to pull me down in the name of Jesus.
58. O Lord, give me vision to recognise good business and customers that come my way in the name of Jesus.
59. O Lord, let my story change, like tree planted by streams of water, in the name of Jesus.
60. Every cloud over my head disturbing my breakthrough, clear away in the name of Jesus.
61. Rulers of darkness in charge of my finance, die in the name of Jesus.
62. Angel of God, break every chain of darkness that tie my business down in the name of Jesus.
63. O Lord, rebuke every power that vow I will end up as a beggar in the name of Jesus.
64. O Lord, make success my inheritance in the name of Jesus.
65. O Lord, silence every power that boast I will not be delivered in the name of Jesus.
66. O Lord silence every power that ask, "where is your God", in the name of Jesus.
67. O Lord, lift up my head for signs and wonders, in the name of Jesus.

68. Holy Ghost, strike the enemy of my breakthrough on the jaw, in the name of Jesus.
69. Holy Ghost, break the teeth of the wicked, troubling my life, in the name of Jesus.
70. O Lord, keep me from anger, so that I may not sin, whenever I see my debtors, in the name of Jesus.
71. Light of God, shine upon me to attract debtors to pay me, in the name of Jesus.
72. Divine oil of God, shine upon me to attract debtors to pay me, in the name of Jesus.
73. O Lord, have mercy on me, save me from the grip of debt, in the name of Jesus.
74. O Lord, deliver me from the hands of those, I have peace with, but do evil to me, in the name of Jesus.
75. On my bed, O Lord, give me wisdom to know step to take, to recover my money, in the name of Jesus.
76. O Lord, make me emperor over my business empire in the name of Jesus.
77. O Lord, I need your presence, don't be far from me, my father and my God, in the name of Jesus.
78. O Lord, keep, my lamb burning, let darkness, be far from me in the name of Jesus.

79. I receive shield of God against advancement of the enemy, in the name of Jesus.

80. O Lord, make me a financial giant in my business in the name of Jesus.

81. O Lord, give me desire of my heart, boil me out of financial mess, debtors want to put me, in the name of Jesus.

82. Let those who trust in chariots fail before me, in the name of Jesus.

83. In your wrath, O Lord, swallow the enemy after my life, in the name of Jesus.

84. O Lord, see me through in this prayer, you are my shepherd I shall not want, in the name of Jesus.

85. O Lord, let your goodness and love overshadow my life, in the name of Jesus.

86. O Lord, the earth is yours, provide and fight for me, in the name of Jesus.

87. O Lord, cleanse me to have clean hands and a pure heart to serve you in the name of Jesus.

88. Oh heaven, scatter enemies that vow to attack me in the name of Jesus.

89. O Lord, let your mercy and love see me through, in the name of Jesus.

90. My eyes are focused on the Lord, my great deliverer, in the name of Jesus.

91. O Lord, do not turn deaf ear to me, answer my prayers and bless me, in the name of Jesus.

92. O Lord, silence enemies assign to drag me on the floor in the name of Jesus.

93. O Lord, I thank you for your love, mercy and protection upon me in this prayer in the name of Jesus.

94. I thank my God, who spared me from going to the grave, in the name of Jesus.

95. I thank my God, who thunders in heaven and answer me by fire, in Jesus name I pray. Amen.

CHAPTER FOUR

LET DARKNESS CLEAR AWAY

Numbers 23:23 "There is no sorcery against Jacob, no divination against Israel. It will now be said of Jacob and of Israel, 'See what God has done!'"

Psalm 112:7. "He will have no fear of bad news; his heart is steadfast, trusting in the Lord."

1. O Lord, clear away every darkness troubling my destiny, in the name of Jesus.
2. Those that boast I will not sing songs of joy in my business, you are a liar, my God shall turn my life around in the name of Jesus.
3. O Lord, let the dread of the enemy be nothing in the name of Jesus.
4. Every battle raised against my finance, scatter in the name of Jesus.
5. Dark powers, assign to stop my breakthrough, die in the name of Jesus.
6. Arrow of affliction fired against my business, backfire in the name of Jesus.
7. Evil counsellor assign to counsel me to failure, die in the name of Jesus.
8. Powers assign to tear my garment by breakthrough die in the name of Jesus.

9. Dark thread that tied my finance to one spot, break and catch fire in the name of Jesus,

10. Soul tie covenant with spirit of debt, break in the name of Jesus.

11. Covenant of darkness attacking the soul of my wealth, break in the name of Jesus.

12. Dark allies that rise up against me in the spirit, scatter in the name of Jesus.

13. Every trap set to catch me, catch your owner in the name of Jesus.

14. Powers that hate my laughter and dance of success, quit my life and die in the name of Jesus.

15. Every curse of darkness pronounced against my finance, backfire to the sender in the name of Jesus.

16. Every cure of darkness pronounced against my destiny, break in the name of Jesus.

17. Every curse of redundancy pronounced against my life, break in the name of Jesus.

18. Every curse of stagnancy operating in my life, break in the name of Jesus.

19. Arrow of debt fired to scatter my marriage, backfire in the name of Jesus.

20. Every prison of my father's house that put my wealth in captivity, break loose, in the name of Jesus.

21. Every power of my father's house covering the glory of my destiny, die in the name of Jesus.

22. Every altar of my father's house assign to swallow my wealth, catch fire and roast to ashes in the name of Jesus.

23. Messenger of darkness against my finance die in the name of Jesus.

24. Powers hat vow the glory of God shall depart from me die in the name of Jesus.

25. Traffic of darkness, diverting poverty to my life, scatter in the name of Jesus.

26. My father and my God, deliver my finance from the hands of the wicked in the name of Jesus.

27. Breakthrough robbers assign to rob me in the spirit, die in the name of Jesus.

28. Destiny robbers assign to steal my star die in the name of Jesus.

29. Progress robbers assign against me release my soul from captivity in the name of Jesus.

30. Ancestral slave traders, trading with my soul in the spirit, die in the name of Jesus.

31. Every satanic slave master, oppressing my soul, die in the name of Jesus.

32. O Lord, turn your hand against enemy f my wealth in the name of Jesus.

33. Dark treaty of brotherhood and sisterhood against my finance, scatter in the name of Jesus.

34. Every enemy of my wealth, I send you on a journey of no return in the name of Jesus.

35. Fire of God, consume every high places of the wicked, fashioned against me, in the name of Jesus.

36. Let the tongue of those hired to prophecy against me, cliff to the roof of their mouth, in the name of Jesus.

37. Every rebellion against me in the spirit, scatter in the name of Jesus.

38. Every rebellion against my finance in my father's house, scatter in the name of Jesus.

39. Every rebellion that emanates from whirlwind against my finance scatter in the name of Jesus.

40. O God arise, separate me form inherited darkness in the name of Jesus.

41. Powers assign to turn my prince to slave be terminated, in the name of Jesus.

42. Any powers that hand me over to dark power for me to be tortured, die in the name of Jesus.

43. Slave master that collects my salary in the spirit, I collect it back by fire, in the name of Jesus.

44. Slave master that refuse to pay, I strike you down with sword of God, and collect it by fire in the name of Jesus.
45. Dark debtors in collaboration with dark devourers against my wealth, die in the name of Jesus.
46. Handwriting of the wicked against my business, be erased in the name of Jesus.
47. Every enemy that rise up against me, scatter in the name of Jesus.
48. O Lord, train my hands for battle to bring down powers of darkness after my life, in the name of Jesus.
49. O Lord, let strangers obey my command, let their heart melt before me, in the name of Jesus.
50. Every gate of darkness erected against me, be pulled down in the name of Jesus.
51. My father and my God, break the bow of the enemy in the name of Jesus.
52. Those that join forces together in order to scatter my finance, shall fail woefully in the name of Jesus.
53. My enemies shall be scattered by strong wind of God, in the name of Jesus.
54. Ruthless men and women after my life shall fail, in the name of Jesus.

55.Let evil recoil on those who rise against me, in the name of Jesus.

56.I shall not live under evil command of the enemy in the name of Jesus.

57.My God shall listen to my prayer and answer me in the name of Jesus.

58.My heart shall not be anguish, in the name of Jesus.

59.My eyes shall look in triumph over my foes, in the name of Jesus.

60.My father and my God, deliver me form all my troubles, in the name of Jesus.

61.I shall not be devoured, as men eat bread, in the name of Jesus.

62.I shall not dwell in the valley of life, in the name of Jesus.

63.My God shall decree victory for me, in the name of Jesus.

64.I am guided and protected by light of God, in the name of Jesus.

65.O Lord, rescue my soul from deceitful and wicked men, in the name of Jesus.

CHAPTER FIVE

O LORD SURPRISE ME

Isaiah 41:15. "See, I will make you into a threshing sledge, new and sharp with many teeth. You will thresh the mountains and crush them, and reduce the hills to chaff."

Numbers 10:35. "Whenever the ark set out, Moses said, "Rise up, O LORD! May your enemies be scattered; may your foes flee before you.""

1. O Lord, appear for me wherever I go in the name of Jesus.
2. O Lord, honour your name and your word in my life, in the name of Jesus.
3. O Lord, release my key of breakthrough to me, in the name of Jesus.
4. O Lord, turn every darkness in my life to light, in the name of Jesus.
5. My ears, hear and understand the word of Holy Spirit, in the name of Jesus.
6. My eyes, see vision and understand it, in the name of Jesus.
7. O Lord, put fear in the heart of my debtors to pay me in the name of Jesus.

8. O Lord, scatter every gang up of debtors to pay me, in the name of Jesus.

9. O Lord, relocate me from Egypt to canaan land of peace and success, in the name of Jesus.

10. O Lord, relocate me from Babylon to Jerusalem of destiny in the name of Jesus.

11. Oh heaven, nullify every curse pronounced against me, in the name of Jesus.

12. Holy Ghost Power, kill powers drinking my wealth, in the name of Jesus.

13. Expected and unexpected source of breakthrough open to my life in the name of Jesus.

14. O Lord, rebuke every pride in my heart, in the name of Jesus.

15. Angels of blessing dedicated o bless me, locate me by fire in the name of Jesus.

16. Angel of my destiny, locate me today, in the name of Jesus.

17. Human angel, dedicated to help me, locate me, in the name of Jesus.

18. My finance in danger, resurrect by fire in the name of Jesus.

19. Every power of incision troubling my finance, die in the name of Jesus.

20. Ark of God, protect my finance, in the name of Jesus.

21. My days of misfortune expire, in the name of Jesus.
22. My delayed blessing, arise, walk to me, in the name of Jesus.
23. Chain of darkness on my neck break and set me free, in the name of Jesus.
24. O Lord, remove veil of darkness in my face that make me trade with wrong people, in the name of Jesus.
25. My father and my God, pronounce debt, dead in my life in the name of Jesus.
26. Rain of blessing and breakthrough fall upon me and kill debt in my life in the name of Jesus.
27. Angels of blessing and breakthrough, my life is available, enter in the name of Jesus.
28. Vehicle of emptiness assign against my wealth, catch fire, in the name of Jesus.
29. Satanic siren scaring my debtors away from paying me, catch fire and roast to ashes, in the name of Jesus.
30. Sudden quarrel between me and my debtors stop by fire, in the name of Jesus.
31. Lord, disgrace unbelievers that go for charm to attack me in the name of Jesus.
32. Every arrow of frustration fired against me backfire in the name of Jesus.

33. Every bewitched account troubling my finance, catch fire and roast to ashes, in the name of Jesus.
34. Any power assign to resurrect spirit of debt in my pocket die in the name of Jesus.
35. Debtors that want to take over my business from me be silenced in the name of Jesus.
36. O Lord, silence untrustworthy fellows around me in the name of Jesus.
37. O Lord, let your rod and staff comfort me in every side of life, in the name of Jesus.
38. O Lord, silence powers assign to multiply my trouble in the name of Jesus.
39. O God arise, crush enemies assign to crush me in the name of Jesus.
40. Let the evil, the enemy conceive and promote consume them in the name of Jesus.
41. I overcome false accusations of detractors and wicked debtors that gang up against me, in the name of Jesus.
42. With God on my side, when the wicked carry out their wicked schemes, they shall fail, in the name of Jesus.
43. Let the path of enemy of my soul be dark and slippery, in the name of Jesus.

44. When men plan to dupe me, my God shall neutralise and nullify, their plans, in the name of Jesus.

45. I shall not be in shame, agony or sorrow, in the name of Jesus.

46. My destiny shall not be covered with darkness, in the name of Jesus.

47. My tongue shall speak breakthrough to my life in the name of Jesus.

48. O Lord, anoint my head for breakthrough and success, in the name of Jesus.

49. O Lord, contend with those who contend with me, in the name of Jesus.

50. O Lord, hide me from the conspiracy of the enemy that vow I shall fail in business, in the name of Jesus.

51. O Lord, expose and disgrace those who shoot from the ambush in the name of Jesus.

52. O Lord, turn every perfect plan of the enemy to nothing in the name of Jesus.

53. O Lord, protect my life from the threat of the enemy in the name of Jesus.

54. In God, my soul will be satisfied as with the richest of foods in the name of Jesus.

55. Angels of God brandish spear and javelin against those who pursue me in the name of Jesus.

56. Every wicked scheme of the enemy against me shall fail in the name of Jesus.
57. With God on my side I will never be shaken in the name of Jesus.
58. O Lord, disgrace who bless with their mouth but curse with their heart in the name of Jesus.
59. With God on my side I will not be shaken, in the name of Jesus.
60. I shall dwell in the house of the Lord and not be shaken, in the name of Jesus.
61. O Lord, disgrace those who conspire against me without offence, in the name of Jesus.
62. O Lord, save me from enemies that hotly pursue me in the name of Jesus.
63. O Lord, prepare a table before me in the presence of my enemies that think I am done with, in the name of Jesus.
64. O Lord, give me strength to seek peace and pursue it, in the name of Jesus.
65. O Lord, give me victory over my enemy in the name of Jesus.
66. People shall not shake their heads at me as sign of pity, in the name of Jesus.

CHAPTER SIX

O LORD EMPOWER MY DEBTORS TO PAY

Psalm 34:10. "The lions may grow weak and hungry but those who seek the Lord lack no good things."

1. O Lord, I thank you that my debtors are alive to do the needful, in the name of Jesus.
2. O Lord, open the ears of my debtors to sermon and call to pay debts they owe, in the name of Jesus.
3. O Lord, open the eyes of my debtors to see reason they should pay me, in the name of Jesus.
4. O lord, give me bold heart to speak to my debtors, in the name of Jesus.
5. O Lord, enlarge the coast of my debtors, to pay what they owe in the name of Jesus.
6. O Lord, build the base of my debtors wealth, in the name of Jesus.
7. O Lord, make way for my debtors and revive their finance in the name of Jesus.
8. O Lord, break every yoke troubling my debtors from paying what they owed me, in the name of Jesus.

9. Cobwebs of poverty in the life of my debtors, catch fire and roast to ashes, in the name of Jesus.

10. Arrow of stagnancy in my life of my debtors, backfire to where you came from, in the name of Jesus.

11. Holy Ghost Power, guide the treasure of my debtors from bankruptcy, in the name of Jesus.

12. Holy ghost Power, confront the problems of my debtors, and set them free in the name of Jesus.

13. I fireback every anti-testimony arrow fired against my debtors to remain stagnant in life, in the name of Jesus.

14. Every stubborn spirit, in the life of my debtors that cause delay to pay me, die in the name of Jesus.

15. Whatever will happen that will make my debtors pay me, happen now in the name of Jesus.

16. O Lord, let my debtors experience testimony of breakthrough and pay me, in the name of Jesus.

17. Powers fighting my debtors in order to stop him from paying me, die in the name of Jesus.

18. Powers hat want the glory of my debtors to die, so that I may lose, shall fail in the name of Jesus.

19. Powers that vow, my debtors shall suffer losses and refuse to pay me, you are a liar, die in the name of Jesus.

20. Every power of impossibility draining the finance of my debtors, die in the name of Jesus.

21. Spirit of bankruptcy in the life of my debtors, die in the name of Jesus.

22. O Lord, release angelic assistance for debtors to pay their debts in the name of Jesus.

23. Every battle older than my debtors holding them from paying me, die in the name of Jesus.

24. Every slaughter house assign to consume my debtor before his/her time, catch fire and roast to ashes.

25. Evil net design to trap my debtors from functioning catch fire and roast to ashes, in the name of Jesus.

26. Evil imagination of debtors against me be nullified in the name of Jesus.

27. Sudden attack on the finance of my debtors, be nullified in the name of Jesus.

28. Arrow of sudden death fired into the family of my debtors, backfire in the name of Jesus.

29. Every sponsored terror confronting my debtors, die in the name of Jesus.

30. Wicked invaders in the finance of my debtors, die in the name of Jesus.

31. Traitors that surround my debtors to fall, scatter in the name of Jesus.

32. Looters working to loot my debtors, be exposed in the name of Jesus.

33. Fear that grip my debtors from paying me, die in the name of Jesus.

34. Every sword of poverty fashion against the financial of my debtors, break in the name of Jesus.

35. Fire of trouble in the life of my debtors, quench in the name of Jesus.

36. Fire of confusion, consume every camp on the way of my debtors, in the name of Jesus.

37. Any power, speaking evil to the heart of my debtors, die in the name of Jesus.

38. My stubborn debtors shall not know peace until I am paid in the name of Jesus.

39. Every blockage on the way of my debtor, clear away in the name of Jesus.

40. Every spirit that discourage my debtor from paying me, die in the name of Jesus.

41. O Lord, open heaven to my debtors to pay me what they owe in the name of Jesus.

42. Any evil association my debtor is a member of, making things difficult for him/her to pay me, scatter in the name of Jesus.

43. My debtor, make me mistake and be expelled in the cult that gives you strength not to pay me, in the name of Jesus.

44. Rain of confusion, fall in the camp of powers supporting my debtors in the name of Jesus.

45. Evil cloud over the head of my debtors, clear away in the name of Jesus.

46. O Lord, give ear to my petition, save me from stubborn debtors that refuse to pay me, in the name of Jesus.

47. Holy Spirit, arrest the heart of debtors that tell lies, and deny owing me, in the name of Jesus.

48. O Lord, remove veil of wickedness on the face of stubborn debtors in my life, in the name of Jesus.

49. Let my word be sweater than honey in the ears of my debtors, to crouse them to pay, in the name of Jesus.

50. Errors I made shall not sink me, I shall walk over it, in the name of Jesus.

51. Enemy shall not silence me in the name of Jesus.

52. Evil powers assign to multiply the trouble of my debtor, meet double failure, in the name of Jesus.

53. Every gang up assign to humiliate my debtors, scatter in the name of Jesus.

54. Powers that advance against my debtors in order to consume them and stop my payment, meet double failure, in the name of Jesus.

55. O Lord, save my debtors from trouble that may engulf them, in the name of Jesus.

56. O Lord, judge the wicked that owe me but go after other gods to attack me, in the name of Jesus.

57. Veil of darkness be removed from the face of my debtors, to pay me and serve God, in the name of Jesus.

58. I speak to the ear of my debtors, hear the word of the Lord, and pay your debt, in the name of Jesus.

59. Defeat that brings sorrow, quit the life of my debtors, to pay me what they owe in the name of Jesus.

60. Holy Spirit, arrest my debtors to pay me, in the name of Jesus.

61. Death shall not feed on my debtors, in the name of Jesus.

62. Wicked deceivers around my debtors, scatter and rise no more in the name of Jesus.

63. Sadness that demoralise life, be erased out of the life of my debtors in the name of Jesus.

64. I and my debtors shall be glad we serve the Lord, in the name of Jesus.

65.O Lord, break the power of the wicked that refuse to pay what they owe in the name of Jesus.

CHAPTER SEVEN

LET SPIRIT OF DEATH BE SILENCED

Psalm 36:4. "Even on his bed he plots evil; he commits himself to a sinful course and does not reject what is wrong."

Psalm 63:9. "They who seek my life will be destroyed; they will go down to the depths of the earth."

1. O Lord, I am a man/woman of unclean lips, cleanse me and forgive me, in the name of Jesus.
2. O lord, give me heart that fights fear and overcome it in the name of Jesus.
3. O Lord, silence spirit of death assign to torment me, in the name of Jesus.
4. O Lord, take my guilt away and atone for my sin, in the name of Jesus.
5. Satanic tax collector assign against me, die in the name of Jesus.
6. O Lord, disgrace and defeat, debtors who traps and snares to consume me, in the name of Jesus.
7. I will not be pulled down from exalted seat in the name of Jesus.

8. Darkness and distress arraigned to consume me, expire in the name of Jesus.

9. My foundation, receive anointing of success, in the name of Jesus.

10. Every root of poverty in my life, wither die, in the name of Jesus.

11. Woe to those who take bribe to sink my finance and naked me, in the name of Jesus.

12. Woe to those who are heroes at doing evil, they shall be trapped in it, in the name of Jesus.

13. Woe to those who are wise in their own eyes to pull down in the race of life, in the name of Jesus.

14. Woe to those who replace good things in my destiny with bad things in order to sink my life, in the name of Jesus.

15. Woe to those who call good evil in order to mislead me and fail in life, in the name of Jesus.

16. Powers assign to plant lack of understanding in me, shall fail in the name of Jesus.

17. Those that boast I will die of hunger shall be the one that will die of hunger, in the name of Jesus.

18. Evil elders that take life at will in my father's house, scatter in the name of Jesus.

19. The blood of my children shall not be used for sacrifice, in the name of Jesus.
20. My blood shall not be used to settle scores in the name of Jesus.
21. Powers assign to drink my blood and eat my flesh as a result of business translation, die in the name of Jesus.
22. Those that seek evil places in order to destroy me, use your head to carry evil load in the name of Jesus.
23. Terror of the dark after my life, die in the name of Jesus.
24. Mourners assign for me by debtors in the spirit, waiting to manifest, die I the spirit, in the name of Jesus.
25. Every spirit of death multiplying my sorrow, die in the name of Jesus.
26. Powers assign to make me bankrupt die in the name of Jesus.
27. Wicked powers raised to plunder me, I silence you in the name of Jesus.
28. Spirit of flirt in my eyes, draining my pocket die in the name of Jesus.
29. Evil money that cause problem in my finance die, in the name of Jesus.
30. Charms that cause problem in my life die, in the name of Jesus.

31. Bloodshed carried out by debtors to destroy my goodwill, meet double failure, in the name of Jesus.

32. Angels of God, slap those who stay up at night to attack me, in the name of Jesus.

33. Power that want me to die before my glory appears, die in the name of Jesus.

34. Those that boast I shall live in the land of the dead shall fail, but see me in mansion of the living, in the name of Jesus.

35. My asset shall not be divided as plunder by the enemy, in the name of Jesus.

36. Every yoke upon me shall break in the name of Jesus.

37. Powers assign to hand me over to cruel master, your time is up, die, in the name of Jesus.

38. Condition that will make me groan and lament, expire in the name of Jesus.

39. Evil net design to trap me down, catch fire and roast to ashes in the name of Jesus.

40. Horror of the day and of the night, my life is not your candidate, die in the name of Jesus.

41. Sword of darkness, fashioned against me, break in the name of Jesus.

42. Every stubborn pursuer after my life, be wasted in the name of Jesus.

43. Wasters assign to waste my life, be wasted in the name of Jesus.

44. Powers confronting me in the spirit to bury my talent and naked me financially, I am not your candidate, therefore, die in the name of Jesus.

45. I pull down and set ablaze every stronghold of the enemy, in the name of Jesus.

46. Evil revolt in the spirit down the brave every stronghold of the enemy in the name of Jesus.

47. O Lord arise, strike down the brave among the wicked against me, in the name of Jesus.

48. O Lord arise, strike down and bury the weak among the wicked that rise up against me, in the name of Jesus.

49. Angels of God, take control of highways the wicked assemble to attack me, in the name of Jesus.

50. Every wicked treaty of the enemy against me, break in the name of Jesus.

51. Murderers in the spirit, assign against my family, die in the name of Jesus.

52. Let powers assign to attack me, miss their way and run mad, in the name of Jesus.

53. Powers that slaughter destiny, my life is not your candidate, die in the name of Jesus.

54. Sword of God, descend in judgement upon enemy of my destiny, in the name of Jesus.

55. No weapon fashion against me shall prosper, in the name of Jesus.

56. False gods consulted to attack me, die in the name of Jesus.

57. Blood thirsty debtors working against my destiny, meet double failure in the name of Jesus.

58. O Lord, heal me, my bones are in anguish, in the name of Jesus.

59. O Lord, deliver me from the hand of debtors that pursue me in order to harm me in the name of Jesus.

60. O God arise, against the rage of the enemy in the name of Jesus.

61. O God, bring to end the violence of the enemy, in the name of Jesus.

62. O Lord, deliver me form those who sharpen sword at me, in the name of Jesus.

63. Every deadly weapon fashion against me, catch fire and burn to ashes in the name of Jesus.

64. O Lord, let those who dig hole and scoop it out fall into the pit dug for me, in the name of Jesus.

65. Powers assign to pull down my star, die in the name of Jesus.

66. Enemies in ambush to kill me, die in the ambush in the name of Jesus.

67. I will not die as a bankrupt man in the name of Jesus.

68. Gate of hell waiting to consume me be pulled down by the thunder of God in the name of Jesus.

69. Though I walk through the valley of the shadow of death, I shall not die, in the name of Jesus.

70. Angels of God, encamp round me and protect me, in the name of Jesus.

71. O Lord, reverse spoken word against me, in the name of Jesus.

72. O Lord, forgive me, I don't want to die a sinner, in the name of Jesus.

73. O Lord, save me from the condemnation of the wicked, in the name of Jesus.

74. My health shall not fail in the name of Jesus.

75. O Lord, protect and preserve me from wickedness of the wicked in the name of Jesus.

76. Every spirit of death after me shall die in the name of Jesus.

CHAPTER EIGHT

I FIRE ENEMIES OF MY WEALTH

Genesis 12:3 "I will bless those who bless you, and whoever curses you I will curse; and all people on earth will be blessed through you."

Psalm 105:14 "He allowed no one to oppress them; for their sake he rebuked kings."

1. O Lord, let the voice, the song , the dance of witchcraft power, expire in the name of Jesus.
2. O Lord, disgrace any power assign to scatter my testimony in the name of Jesus.
3. O Lord, silence every debtor that consult mediums and spirits I order to harm me, in the name of Jesus.
4. O Lord, break every rod of oppression stretched at me, in the name of Jesus.
5. Every yoke of debt upon my shoulder, break in the name of Jesus.
6. Every barricade on my way of success, catch fire and roast to ashes, in the name of Jesus.
7. Poverty dream tormenting my destiny, expire in the name of Jesus.
8. Spirit of poverty after my wealth, die in the name of Jesus.

9. Powers that lock door of blessings against me, die in the name of Jesus.
10. Evil embargo placed upon my wealth, break and scatter, in the name of Jesus.
11. Altar of darkness on evil mat chanting evil against me, die in your mat in the name of Jesus.
12. Witch doctor, hired to scatter my finance, your time is up, die in the name of Jesus.
13. Evil priest on mission to scatter my finance, die in the name of Jesus.
14. Wicked arrow fired against my finance, backfire in the name of Jesus.
15. My source of finance, blocked by the enemy, be released from bondage of darkness, in the name of Jesus.
16. Limitation in my foundation blocking my finance, die in the name of Jesus.
17. Stubborn pursuer that refuse to turn back from pursuing me, let the earth open and consume you, in the name of Jesus.
18. Every power that pursue me and is now after my debtors, you are rebuked, die in the name of Jesus.
19. Every habit in me that scatter wealth, die in the name of Jesus.

20. Every curse of profitless hard work issued against me backfire, in the name of Jesus.
21. Powers of my father's house that steal my potentials, die in the name of Jesus.
22. Powers that boast I will not make it die, in the name of Jesus.
23. Powers assign to disgrace me in the midst of friends, die in the name of Jesus.
24. Powers assign to disgrace me in my neighbourhood, die in the name of Jesus.
25. Every battle that refuse to go, die in the name of Jesus.
26. Secret place of my father's house, firing arrow of failure into my life, catch fire and roast to ashes, in the name of Jesus.
27. The evil that men do shall come over them in the name of Jesus.
28. Day of disaster, set aside to consume my wealth, expire in the name of Jesus.
29. Those that leave their homes to take over mine, shall fail in the name of Jesus.
30. Foundational battle against my source of wealth, die in the name of Jesus.
31. Witchcraft feast upon my wealth, seize to operate, in the name of Jesus.
32. Enemies assign to attack me, be exposed and be defeated in the name of Jesus.

33. Powers assign to strip me naked in the dream, I strip you naked, therefore, die in the name of Jesus.

34. Traitors that rise up against me, I fire you, die, in the name of Jesus.

35. Dark locusts after my harvest die in the name of Jesus.

36. Powers and personalities assign to extort me in the spirit in order to naked me, die in the name of Jesus.

37. Spirit birds assign to feed on my wealth, die in the name of Jesus.

38. Every dark plantation growing in the garden of my life, troubling my finance, dry up in the name of Jesus.

39. O Lord, be my stronghold in time of trouble, in the name of Jesus.

40. O Lord, pull out the hidden ones, where they hid to attack me, in the name of Jesus.

41. O Lord, cancel the prosperity of debtors that vow will pull my business down, in the name of Jesus.

42. O Lord, disgrace debtors that boast, "nothing will happen, if I don't pay".

43. O Lord, judge every debtor that boast, "I am happy, my creditors are in trouble", in the name of Jesus.

44. Holy Ghost Power, slap debtors whose mouth is full of lies and threat, in the name of Jesus.
45. O Lord, do not reject me or forsake me, in the name of Jesus.
46. False witness that rise against me, be silenced in the name of Jesus.
47. In time of famine, I shall not beg before I feed, but enjoy in plenty in the name of Jesus.
48. Holy Ghost, torture and disgrace the wicked that borrow but refuse to pay, in the name of Jesus.
49. I fire any power assign to drain my anointing in the name of Jesus.
50. Every arrow fired against my source of wealth, backfire in the name of Jesus.
51. Any power that wants me to live with a broken heart shall fail to realise it, in the name of Jesus.
52. I fire arrow in the midst of enemies that rise against me, in the name of Jesus.
53. All those against me, my God shall charge you with crime upon crimes, in the name of Jesus.
54. O Lord, let your fierce anger overtake my enemies in the name of Jesus.
55. I shall not be cast away at old age in the name of Jesus.
56. Heavenly vehicle of God, crush enemy of my destiny to powder, in the name of Jesus.

57. Every evil axe wielded against me, break in the name of Jesus.

58. Every affliction targeted against me shall backfire in the name of Jesus.

59. O Lord, comfort me on every side in the name of Jesus.

60. I shall enjoy love and sympathy of God, in the name of Jesus.

61. O Lord my God, make me flourish in the name of Jesus.

62. My God shall not surrender me to the desire of my foes, in the name of Jesus.

63. O Lord, put new song in my mouth, in the name of Jesus

CHAPTER NINE

MY FINANCE SHALL NOT SCATTER

Psalm 69:4 "Those who hate me without reason outnumber the hairs of my head; many are my enemies without cause, those who seek to destroy me. I am forced to restore what I did not steal."

Micah 7:8 "Do not gloat over me, my enemy! Though I have fallen, I will rise. Though I sit in darkness, the LORD will be my light."

1. O Lord, don't hide your face from me, but bless me in the name of Jesus.
2. O Lord, rebuke powers assign to scatter my finance, in the name of Jesus.
3. O Lord, give me abundance of milk and honey in the spirit, in the name of Jesus.
4. O Lord, silence every power assign to slave me naked in the name of Jesus.
5. Every warfare of the enemy against my finance, scatter in the name of Jesus.
6. Powers using the night to attack and scatter my breakthrough, your time is up, die in the name of Jesus.
7. My heart afflicted by evil debtors be healed in the name of Jesus.

8. Any personality, living with me but inflicting me with arrow of debt, your time is up, be exposed and be disgraced in the name of Jesus.

9. Spirit of dustbin living in my life, come out and die, in the name of Jesus.

10. Every rebellion against my finance in the sea, scatter in the name of Jesus.

11. Debtors that are burden in my life, O Lord, create fear in them to pay me, in the name of Jesus.

12. Every siege against my finance, scatter in the name of Jesus.

13. Strangers and visitors that drop strange material in my house in order to make me bankrupt, let your arrow go back and consume you in the name of Jesus.

14. People I reveal the secret of my business to, but now attacking me, be exposed and be disgraced in the name of Jesus.

15. Spiritual sore in my mouth, scaring helpers away, be healed in the name of Jesus.

16. Angel of my destiny, locate me by fire, and favour me, in the name of Jesus.

17. O Lord my father urn my life to bigger testimony in the name of Jesus.

18. O Lord, enlarge my financial coast by fire in the name of Jesus.

19. Powers assign to marry me to debt, my life is not your candidate die in the name of Jesus.
20. Conversations in the past, now troubling my finance , die in the name of Jesus.
21. Evil elders, that vow to scatter my finance, die in the name of Jesus.
22. Devourers in the spirit assign to devour my wealth, die in the name of Jesus.
23. Those that rise to plunder my treasure die in the name of Jesus.
24. I advance against the gate of the wicked, I pull it down and possess my possession, in the name of Jesus.
25. My environment hear the word of the Lord, and vomit my wealth in the name of Jesus.
26. Powers that naked people in my father's house, that says, it is my turn to be naked, I am not your candidate die in the name of Jesus.
27. Those that give bribes in order to molest me and refuse to pay me, be disgraced, in the name of Jesus.
28. Dark harvester, assign to harvest my breakthrough in the spirit, die in the name of Jesus.
29. Powers assign to count me guilty before my debtors, die in the name of Jesus.

30. I decree against every mountain fashioned against my finance, in the name of Jesus.

31. Every evil arrow fired by wicked debtors against me, by wicked debtors, in order to stop me from collecting my money, backfire to the sender, in the name of Jesus.

32. Dark locus after my harvest and gain, die in the name of Jesus.

33. Wicked judgement against my finance and business, scatter in the name of Jesus.

34. Dark power assign to resurrect spirit of poverty in bank account, die in the name of Jesus.

35. Powers assign to bring me low as mat for enemy to walk on, die in the name of Jesus.

36. My virtues in the warehouse of darkness, I recover you in the name of Jesus.

37. Enemy shall not turn the garden of my life, to wasteland in the name of Jesus.

38. Evil gift I received in the spirit, working against my finance catch fire and roast to ashes in the name of Jesus.

39. Evil gift I received from people now working against my destiny, die in the name of Jesus.

40. Evil revolt against me in the spirit scatter in the name of Jesus.

41. Every idol of my father's house against my success die in the name of Jesus.

42. Inherited poverty in my lineage, troubling my finance, die in the name of Jesus.

43. Evil eyes monitoring me for evil, go blind in the name of Jesus.

44. Dark mirror from the pit of hell, monitoring my destiny, break in the name of Jesus.

45. Power giving me evil command, die in the name of Jesus.

46. Holy Ghost Fire, burn to ashes every filthy rag presented to me in the spirit, in the name of Jesus.

47. Never again will I record loss in my business and career in the name of Jesus.

48. Former things that don't promote success, your time is up, die in the name of Jesus.

49. Every planned revenge against me scatter in the name of Jesus.

50. I break the arm of the wicked assign to scatter my business, in the name of Jesus.

51. Whirlwind shall not unseat me in my place of work or business in the name of Jesus.

52. Whirlwind of darkness, assign to blow my business away in the spirit, die in the name of Jesus.

53. O Lord, let the way of the wicked against my finance perish, in the name of Jesus.

54. Evil pot raised against my finance break in the name of Jesus.

55. O Lord, reveal debtors whose mouth cannot be trusted, in the name of Jesus.

56. O Lord, deliver me from debt I cant account for, in the name of Jesus.

57. O Lord, let the weep in my face dry, put smiles in my face, in the name of Jesus.

58. Debts that makes e weak and my eyes weak with sorrow receive divine solution, in the name of Jesus.

59. O Lord, do judgement to those who steal from me without cause in the name of Jesus.

60. Let the wicked be ensnared by the work of their hands in the name of Jesus.

61. O Lord, lift me out o the pit of poverty in the name of Jesus.

62. Destructive forces against my finance, die in the name of Jesus.

63. Horror staring at me to discourage me form shining die in the name of Jesus.

64. Those that plan for my fall shall fail woefully in the name of Jesus.

65. Friends that attack me in secret be exposed and be disgraced in the name of Jesus.

66. O Lord, deliver me from enemy whose tongue is against my finance in the name of Jesus.

67. Let my enemies vanish like water that flows away in the name of Jesus.
68. O Lord, confuse the enemy that plan evil against me, in the name of Jesus.

CHAPTER TEN

I SHALL NOT BE POOR.

Psalm 113:7 "He raises the poor from the dust and lifts the needy from the ash heap."

Isaiah 43: 18-19. "18. Forget the former things; do not dwell on the past. 19. See, I am doing a new thing! Now it springs up; do you not perceive it? I am making a way in the desert and streams in the wasteland."

1. O Lord, provoke my destiny with miracles of breakthroughs in the name of Jesus.
2. O Lord, give me miracle that will surprise me, in the name of Jesus.
3. O Lord, double my miracle in the name of Jesus.
4. O Lord, muster your army of war and scatter my enemies in the name of Jesus.
5. O Lord, let terror and fear seize the heart of my enemy, in the name of Jesus.
6. O Lord, pronounce good health into my life, in the name of Jesus.
7. O Lord, let agent of famine from the pit of hell fashion against my soul die in the name of Jesus.

8. O Lord, let joy and gladness be my food in the name of Jesus.

9. O Lord, move on my behalf, lift me up when I am cast down, in the name of Jesus.

10.I shall be celebrated and not be mocked, in the name of Jesus.

11.Wicked and ungodly people around me, be exposed and be disgraced in the name of Jesus.

12.Whatever fuel fire of debt in my life, die in the name of Jesus.

13.Snail anointing operating in my life, dry up in the name of Jesus.

14.Evil arrow fired against my miracle, backfire in the name of Jesus.

15.Evil arrow fired against my destiny backfire in the name of Jesus.

16.Any power manipulating my account in the spirit, die in the name of Jesus.

17.Every incantation on the sand to discourage debtors o pay me, backfire, in the name of Jesus.

18.Open disgrace meant for me, my life is not for you, scatter in the name of Jesus.

19.Witchcraft bag collecting my money, vomit it to me, and catch fire, in the name of Jesus.

20.I pull of garment of failure in my body, in the name of Jesus.

21. I command every devourer assign against my life in order to naked me, be put to shame, in the name of Jesus.

22. Those who tell lies to gain way into my life in order to naked me, be put to shame, in the name of Jesus.

23. Those that wickedness burns like fire in their heart, be consumed by it in the name of Jesus.

24. Those who plan, I shall remain a reminants, you are not my God, die in the name of Jesus.

25. Those that decree destruction and failure shall be my portion will fail, in the name of Jesus.

26. Those who wickedly refuse to pay me, be placed in captivity in the name of Jesus.

27. Those who rise to frustration my plans, shall fail woefully in the name of Jesus.

28. Those who display demonic knowledge day after day to scatter my plans shall fail in the name of Jesus.

29. Those who display demonic knowledge night after night to defraud me shall fail, in the name of Jesus.

30. Those whose hands are wicked schemes shall not find me as target in the name of Jesus.

31. Those that harbour malice in the heart against me shall be put to shame, in the name of Jesus.

32. Those I lend freely but turn back to pay me with evil shall be disgraced, in the name of Jesus.

33. Those that refuse to turn from evil and do good, o Lord, judge them, in the name of Jesus.

34. Those seeking my life for the favour and good I do to them, O Lord, disgrace them in the name of Jesus.

35. Those that pray I shall die, and my name will perish, use your head to carry it, in the name of Jesus.

36. Those who dug pit for me, shall fall into the pit they dug for me, in the name of Jesus.

37. Those that wait with plans to divide my wealth, scatter in the name of Jesus.

38. Those that vow I will not see helpers anywhere I go, you are not my creator die in the name of Jesus.

39. Those who want me to be in pain, replace me and die in the name of Jesus.

40. Those who seek my life, shall be put to shame in the name of Jesus.

41. Those who clothe themselves with violence against me shall fail in the name of Jesus.

42. Those that want me to languish in poverty, replace me and die in the name of Jesus.

43. Every curse of poverty, break in the name of Jesus.

44. Every covenant with poverty, break in the name of Jesus .

45. Holy Ghost Power, break and scatter gate of darkness that held me captive, in the name of Jesus.

46. I speak against anger that brings poverty to life, in the name of Jesus.

47. Voice of the wicked against my business and career be nullified in the name of Jesus.

48. I shall not be found where disaster strikes, in the name of Jesus.

49. Every plan to sell me out to enemy shall fail in the name of Jesus.

50. Those who plots destruction for me shall be consumed by it, in the name of Jesus.

51. Every cult activity assign to pull me down, scatter in the name of Jesus.

52. My account shall not be bewitched in the name of Jesus.

53. My financial record shall not go in flame in the spirit in the name of Jesus.

54. Floodwaters of darkness shall not sweep me away in the name of Jesus.

55. I shall not be treated as alien by my helpers in the name of Jesus.

56. I will not restore what I did not steal in the name of Jesus.

57. I am saved from the hands of those who hate me without cause in the name of Jesus.

58. My eyes shall not fail in the name of Jesus.

59. I shall not sink in the battle of life, in the name of Jesus.

60. I command enemy that occupy my seat to flee in the name of Jesus.

61. My God shall pour rain of blessing upon me in the name of Jesus.

62. My God shall be gracious to me and bless me in the name of Jesus.

63. My God shall restore my fortunes in the name of Jesus.

64. O Lord, set my feet on the rock of God, in the name of Jesus.

CHAPTER ELEVEN

I CLAIM MY WEALTH BY FIRE

Psalm 72:9 "The desert tribes will bow before him and his enemies will lick the dust."

1. Oh heavens, hear me, touch the heart of debtors to pay me in the name of Jesus.
2. Listen Oh earth, vomit what belongs to me in the name of Jesus.
3. Listen oh earth and heaven, let no man cheat me, in the name of Jesus .
4. Listen oh earth, let strangers with my wealth release it to me by fire, in the name of Jesus.
5. Any power anywhere, standing between me and God's prophecy for my life, die in the name of Jesus.
6. O Lord, let me receive divine encounter with you, in the name of Jesus.
7. O Lord, visit my destiny and bless me, in the name of Jesus.
8. O Lord, reposition me as lender among leaders in the nation, in the name of Jesus.
9. I will live in the splendour of His majesty, in the name of Jesus.
10. My wealth in the valley of life, come out and locate me in the name of Jesus.

11. Strangers with my wealth, surrender it by fire and I claim it by fire, in the name of Jesus.

12. I reclaim my wealth lost to evil burial fashion against me, in the name of Jesus.

13. I recover all I lost in the past to dark rebels in the name of Jesus.

14. I recover my wealth swallowed by evil altar of my father's house, in the name of Jesus.

15. I reject breakthrough paralysis in my business and career, in the name of Jesus.

16. I possess my foreign benefits in the name of Jesus.

17. My glory, my glory, why are you sleeping when others are shinning? Wake up and shine, in the name of Jesus.

18. Supernatural manifestation, appear in my business in the name of Jesus.

19. Let signs and wonders become inevitable in my life, in the name of Jesus.

20. My head, reject poverty, in the name of Jesus.

21. My hands, reject poverty, in the name of Jesus.

22. My legs, reject poverty, in the name of Jesus.

23. I shall drink wine of joy and swim in breakthrough, in the name of Jesus.

24. Anointing that draw helpers of breakthrough to people, flow in my life, in the name of Jesus.

25. My star shall not go down, but rise and experience breakthrough, in the name of Jesus.

26. This year shall not start or end in bitterness for me, but joy and breakthrough, in the name of Jesus.

27. Today, and forever more, I shall fellowship with God, in happiness with breakthrough songs in my mouth, in the name of Jesus.

28. Wealth that adds honour and splendour to life be my portion, in the name of Jesus.

29. I claim wealth of majesty, in the name of Jesus.

30. I pull of garment of failure and wear garment of breakthrough, in the name of Jesus.

31. I push enemy of my glory aside and claim my glory

32. My head, reject poverty, in the name of Jesus.

33. My financial base, receive anointing of success, in the name of Jesus.

34. Wasteland in the spirit, turn to land that flows with milk and honey in the name of Jesus.

35. I command rain of wealth upon my life, in the name of Jesus.

36. I shall raise my voice and shout for joy to the Lord Almighty for granting me heavenly blessings in the name of Jesus.

37. Neither me or my wealth shall waste away, in the name of Jesus.

38. My mountain top of blessing appear in the name of Jesus.

39. My situation, move from lamentation to glory, in the name of Jesus.

40. I shall not engage in unprofitable venture in the name of Jesus.

41. My trade with poverty and loss is over in the name of Jesus.

42. Whichever direction I turn, I will locate my blessing and breakthrough in the name of Jesus.

43. Whichever direction I go, I will locate helpers that will turn my life around for good, in the name of Jesus.

44. I claim spirit of the noble, to do noble things that bring blessings, in the name of Jesus.

45. I receive spirit of financial discipline in the name of Jesus.

46. O Lord, let I do yield fruits in season, in the name of Jesus.

47. O lord, prosper me and multiply my wealth to your glory, in the name of Jesus.

48. By word of prophecy, my glory shall not turn to shame, in the name of Jesus.

49. By word of prophecy, my God shall keep me off from shame and disgrace in the name of Jesus.

50. By word of prophecy, my persecutors shall be put to shame, in the name of Jesus.

51. By word of prophecy, I break every bond with poverty in the name of Jesus.

52. By word of prophecy, I shall cross over from poverty to breakthrough, in the name of Jesus.

53. By word of prophecy, I command every embargo placed upon my business and career to break in the name of Jesus.

54. By word of prophecy, what I lost in the past I recover you in the name of Jesus.

55. By word of prophecy, my past troubles are over, they shall not rise against in the name of Jesus.

56. By word of prophecy, kindness of God shall fill my home and promote my business in the name of Jesus.

57. By word of prophecy, my business/career shall not end up in ashes, in the name of Jesus.

58. By word of prophecy, I receive double portion of breakthrough, in the name of Jesus.

59. By word of prophecy, word of wisdom and knowledge shall fill my mouth in the name of Jesus.

60. By word of prophecy, my prayer and fasting shall not be in vain in the name of Jesus.

61. By word of prophecy, I receive strength and wisdom to enter and be with the nobles, in the name of Jesus.

62. By word of prophecy, those who owe me, shall pay me, in the name of Jesus.

63. By word of prophecy, every gang up against me shall scatter, in the name of Jesus.

64. By word of prophecy, my God shall enlarge my coast in the name of Jesus.

65. By word of prophecy, my empire of wealth shall not be in ruin, in the name of Jesus.

66. By word of prophecy, debtors shall not put me to shame in the name of Jesus.

67. By word of prophecy, my debtor's heart shall be touched to pay me, in the name of Jesus.

68. By word of prophecy, my God shall make success my inheritance, in the name of Jesus.

69. By word of prophecy, fear is gone in my heart, I shall lie down and sleep in peace, in the name of Jesus.

70. By word of prophecy, my God shall protect me from evil arrow in the name of Jesus.

71. By word of prophecy, every persecution of the enemy against me shall scatter in the name of Jesus.

72.By word of prophecy, I shall be more precious than gold in the eyes of my debtors, in the name of Jesus.

73.By word of prophecy, I shall not be a financial crawler, but a financial giant in the name of Jesus.

74.By word of prophecy, my hope shall not perish in the name of Jesus.

75.By word of prophecy, I shall lie down in green pastures and shall not want, in the name of Jesus.

76.By word of prophecy, I am full of joy and happiness in the name of Jesus.

77.By word of prophecy, the Lord is with me, I will not be shaken, in the name of Jesus.

78.By word of prophecy, my wailing shall turn to dance and joy, in the name of Jesus.

79.By word of prophecy, my financial wounds are healed in the name of Jesus.

80.By word of prophecy, my life shall not be in anguish in the name of Jesus.

81.By word of prophecy, my strength shall not fail in the name of Jesus.

82.By word of prophecy, I shall not be forgotten while I am alive, in the name of Jesus.

YOU HAVE BATTLES TO WIN
TRY THESE BOOKS

1. COMMAND THE DAY: DAILY PRAYER BOOK

Each day of the week is loaded with meanings and divine assurance. God did not create each day of the week for the fun of it. Blessings, success, gifts, resources, hopes, portfolios, duties, rights, prophecies, warnings and challenges, are loaded in each day.

Do you know the language, command or decree you can use to claim what belongs to you in each day of the week? Do you know in Christendom, Monday can be equated to one of the days of creation in Genesis chapter one? Do you know creation lasted for six days and God rested on the seventh day? What day of the week can Christian equate as the first day of the week, if we follow Christian calendar? What day can we call day seven?

This book shall give insight to these questions. It shall explain how you can command each day of the week according to creation in the book of Genesis chapter one.

Above all, you shall exercise your right and claim what is hidden in each day of the week.
Check for this in COMMAND THE DAY: DAILY PRAYER BOOK

2. PRAYER TO REMEMBER DREAMS

A lot of people are passing through this spiritual epidemic on a daily basis. Their dream life is epileptic, having no ability to remember all dreams they dream, or sometimes forget everything entirely. This is nothing but spiritual havoc you need to erase from your spiritual record.
The answer to every form of spiritual blackout caused by spiritual erasers is found in, PRAYER TO REMEMBER DREAMS

3. 100% CONFESSIONS AND PROPHECIES TO LOCATE HELPERS AND HELPERS TO LOCATE YOU

This is a wonderful book on confessions and prophecies to locate helpers and helpers to locate you. It is a prayer book loaded with over two thousand (2,000) prayer points.

The book unravels how to locate unknown helpers, prayers to arrest mind of helpers and prayers for manifestation after encounter with helpers.

4. ANOINTING FOR ELEVENTH HOUR HELP: HOPE AND HELP FOR YOUR TURBULENT TIMES

This book tells much of what to do at injury hour called eleventh hour. When you read and use this book as prescribed fear shall vanish in your life when pursuing a project, career or contract.

5. PRAYER TO LOCATE HELPERS AND HELPERS TO LOCATE YOU

Our divine helper is God. He created us to be together and be of help to one another. In the midst of no help we lost out, ending our journey in the wilderness.

There are keys assign to open right doors of life. You need right key to locate your helpers. Enough is enough; of suffering in silence.

With this book, you shall locate your helpers while your helpers shall locate you.

6. FIRE FOR FIRE PART ONE: (PRAYER BOOK BOOK 1)

This prayer book is fast at answering spiritual problems. It is a bulldozer prayer book, full of prayers all through. It is highly recommended for night vigil. Testimonies are pouring in daily from users of this book across the world!

7. PRAYER FOR FRUIT OF THE WOMB: EXPECTING MOTHERS

This prayer book is children magnet. By faith and believe in God Almighty, as soon as you use this book open doors to child bearing shall be yours. Amen

8. PRAYER FOR PREGNANT WOMEN: WITH ALL CHRISTIAN NAMES AND MEANINGS

This is a spiritual prayer book loaded with prayers of solution for pregnant women. As soon as you take in, the prayers you shall pray from day one of conception to the day of delivery are written in this book.

9. <u>WARFARE IN THE OFFICE: PRAYER TO SILENCE TOUGH TIMES IN OFFICE</u>

It is high time you pray prayers of power must change hands in office. Use this book and liberate yourself from every form of office yoke.

10. <u>MY MARRIAGE SHALL NOT BREAK: THE SECRET TO LOVE AND MARRIAGE THAT LASTS</u>

Marriage is corner piece of life, happiness and joy. You need to hold it tight and guide it from wicked intruders and destroyer of homes.

11. <u>VICTORY OVER SATANIC HOUSE PART ONE: RIDDING YOUR HOME OF SPIRITUAL DARKNESS</u>

Are you a tenant, Land lord bombarded left and right, front and back by wicked people around you?
With this book you shall be liberated from the hooks of the enemy.

12. <u>DICTIONARY OF DREAMS: THE DREAM INTERPRETATION</u>

DICTIONARY WITH SYMBOLS, SIGNS, AND MEANINGS

This is a must book for every home. It gives accurate details to about **10,000 (Ten thousand) dreams and interpretations,** written in alphabetical order for quick reference and easy digestion. The book portrays spiritual revelations with sound prophetic guidelines. It is loaded with Biblical references and violent prayers.
Ask for yours today.

For Further Enquiries Contact
THE AUTHOR
EVANGELIST TELLA OLAYERI
P.O. Box 1872 Shomolu Lagos.
Tel: 08023583168

FROM AUTHOR'S DESK

BEFORE YOU GO

Hello,

Thank you for purchasing this book. Would you consider posting a review about this book? In addition to providing feedback and arousing others into Christ's bosom, reviews can help other customers to know about the book.

Please take a minute to leave a review on this book.

I would appreciate that!

Thank you in advance, for your review and your patronage!!

Feel free to drop us your prayer request. We will join faith with you and God's power will be released in your life and issue in question.

http://tellaolayeri.com/prayerrequest.php

NOTE: You can get all my books from my website http://tellaolayeri.com

GOOD NEWS!!!

My audiobook is now available, to get one visit acx.com and search **"Tella Olayeri."**

Brethren, to be loaded and reloaded visit: amazon.com/author/tellaolayeri for a full spiritual sojourn for my books.

Thanks.